POSSIBLE CROCODILES

POSSIBLE CROCODILES

Poems by Barry Marks

BRICK ROAD
POETRY PRESS

Grateful acknowledgment is made to the editors of the following publications in which several of these poems first appeared: *Legal Studies Forum*, *Birmingham Arts Journal*, *Right Hand Pointing* (online) and the anthologies *Poems from the Big Table* and *Einstein at the Odeon Café* (www.churndashpress.com).

Cover photo: © Joe Klune | Dreamstime.com

Author photo: © Barry C Altmark Photography

Brick Road logo by Dwight New

Library of Congress Control Number: 2011929329
ISBN-13: 978-0-9835304-0-4

Published by Brick Road Poetry Press
P. O. Box 751
Columbus, GA 31902-0751

www.brickroadpoetrypress.com

For

Jennifer

Leah

Lauren

Noah

You make life worth living

With special thanks to The Big Table Poets, to Mom 'n Dad and to Colonel E.G. Piper as representative of all the teachers who taught me to love the sound, feel and magic of the English language.

CONTENTS

Teaching the Angels to Dance

The wings, that's the worst problem.
Their wings scrape the carpet and trip
cherubim and seraphim alike until,

with a snort that somehow
hangs musical in the air,
they shoot to the ceiling for a breather.

"Listen to the beat," I plead, but
drum and bass seem to pass through them.
They are lost in melody.
Michael closes his eyes and
unconsciously takes off;
he bumps his head on the chandelier,
settles back to the floor,
blushing, shrugs an apology.

Raphael stumbles into the china cabinet,
Tzaphkiel and Tzadkiel collide,
Metatron practically somersaults over the sofa,
and none of them able to translate their innate grace,
their light-drenched, aerodynamic beauty,
into the simplest of steps.
I joke that perhaps I should find them a pin,
but that falls flat before empty, beatific smiles.

Only Death seems to get it right,
the perfect partner, following my lead,
her dark eyes glowing,
her balance flawless as

she twirls and spins so light on her feet,
she makes me feel like Fred Astaire—

until Gabriel cuts in
with a whisper that this is one dance
I should probably sit out.

There Is Nothing Oppressive
As a Good Man

There is nothing oppressive as a good man
      who has already thought of everything you are feeling
      who is there for you at the end of the line
      who politely prolongs by thinking about something
else and wants you to hold still goddamnit so he can fix you.
      Who denies himself everything you need.

There is nothing oppressive as a good woman
      who cares and cares and cares
      who wants to be everything you should want
      who knows that she is always right and is perfectly
willing to admit that you are, too.
      Who denies herself everything you need.

They do not want to be a bother, to intrude on
      the body in which you are embedded.
They do not want to take anything you have
      until you cannot take it anymore.
They lie awake next to you, petrified with fear
      of lesser men and women, then rise
      to the insistent morning light,
      clutching your future and floating away,
      calling your name quietly so as not to wake you.

The Lion Sleeps (Better) Tonight

Lion got into therapy because he had
issues, mostly aggression control
but also feelings of inadequacy since
the day he learned that tigers were
larger. He's doing ok, but I'm afraid
shark's marriage went aground
despite years of counseling.
His wife complains that he's still
a cold fish.

Giraffe won't speak,
rhino refuses to wear her glasses
and strikes out blindly at everyone,
zebra can't work, and boa still
approaches every hunt as a potential
crushing defeat, but

elephant is doing fine in the twelve-step
program he started the morning after
he gambled away one of his tusks,
and I am pleased to report that mandrill
has been sober for seven months.

Every day he recites the serenity prayer,
goes to his meetings
("Hello, I'm Mandrill. . . ."),
stays away from fermented bananas
and has even stopped worrying
about the size and color of his behind.

So I guess there's hope for us all.

Song

this is not a song
it is a poem about a song
or about something about
a song

you know the one, it goes
da da da dum da de da
that one
or another one maybe

it doesn't matter really
you choose the song
close your eyes
clear your thoughts
and let the song start

that one
now you will hear it
the rest of the day
I hope it's one you like
and not one your six year-old
sings over and over
or the theme song
for your wife's religion

I hope it is your song
your best song
a song so true to you
you could have written it yourself

that song is the one I mean
the one I write about

the one that tells you
there is more to you
than blood and snot
more than money and words
more than the four corners of your body
there is something that can last
there is a God
and He can carry a tune

I Stop to Ponder the Stentorian Colors of the Day

The railing down from the deck
to the garbage cans was wobbly, and
since you left, I've certainly had
time on my hands,
so I unretired my rusty box saw,
found an old two-by-four
and some three penny nails
and got to work.

A dog was barking, yelling his name
at the dog next door,
Big Dog Who Swims! Big Dog Who Swims!
To which his neighbor barked back,
Dog Who Hates Cats! and
some nearby mutt yapped,
Mama's Favorite! Mama's Favorite!

A cardinal was shouting,
Beauty! A mockingbird said
the same, of course.

A chameleon shot out of the hedge,
stopped by my foot and, turning from green
to almost-brown, sneered,
You can't see me, then skittered off.

The sky was whispering until
I looked up, and it screamed,
Forever!
to which the grass responded,
Joy is fragile!

And the saw
sang in my hands
and the wood?
Come on, now. An old two-by-four
with a bent nail in its heart?
Everyone knows dead wood
has nothing to say.

Uprising

Coyote, or maybe a fox, he had no place
in the woods between our deck and
our neighbor's new swimming pool,
but there he was, trotting off
like he was surveying his backyard,
tail swaggering between the brambles.

What if he is the advance scout
for a war party, the dispossessed
risen to reclaim their birthright?
He will return with others of his kind
and bear, boar, bison
bent on driving us back to the city.

They will attack just before dawn,
led, no doubt, by a reconnaissance squad
of bats squeaking the coordinates.
The attackers will set up perimeters
(squirrels should make superb sentries)
and a mobile HQ atop the water tower.
A gaggle of geese will provide air cover,
sacrificing themselves into F-16 intakes and
Apache blades when the National Guard counterattacks.

Perhaps they will enlist allies
among the insect world: roaches, flies
and spiders putting off their internecine conflict
to unite against the poisoning, heavy-footed foe;
or worse, they will send emissaries
to the ghost-shirted assassins,
microbes, bacilli and fungi,
the mutating viral horde,

to sweep off their reservations
and attack with lethal bio-weaponry.

Olde Weatherly will fall to the insurrectionists,
then New Weatherly and the nameless
office park across the street.
They will reclaim 665 Weatherly Lane.
Vines will violate our precious possessions,
choking Beanie Babies and Barbies,
evicting Monet prints from our walls.
A family of armadillos will nest
in the master bath,
while deer doze in our bed
and a solitary opossum
sways in my hammock.

The occupying force
will forage the pantry,
Shermanizing,
animal bummers, loaded down
with Fritos and Fruit Roll-ups,
scurrying into the wild night.

They will eat my daughter's loyalist dog;
I assume the cats
will quickly turn coat.

As a final indignity, some furry lockpick
will free our parakeets
to soar out the shattered bay window
into the spring air, their wings
stretched in unfettered glory,
celebrating the joy
of the undomesticated sun.

The Engineer's Reward

The little man in the frumpy suit
(I think it's called *tweed*)
was bubbling with excitement as he
showed me around the shop.
Each massive machine was beautiful,
no, more than that, *artistic*,
ancient, Byzantine, somehow alive;
all shiny steel and brass and, I swear,
silver and gold and growing cedar;
wheels, cogs and limbs
perfectly balanced.

No dirt, no soot, not a drop of oil,
perfect tolerances; no grinding except
where grinding seemed part of
the process.

The wave machine, wide as
my house, worked
about the way you'd expect,
but produced much more than water.
The next unit was larger still.
"Gravity," his eyes twinkled.
"Perhaps the most important of all."
He showed me how the Light Extruder
and Timestamp all fed off the Gravity Gizmo,
each ray, each nanosecond pushed
or pulled along as the gears and flywheels
spun and whirred.
We walked past a door marked
"Life" and he shook his head.
"Perhaps later."

"No computers?" I asked.
He scowled. "In the basement.
The other guy uses 'em."
"Fuel?"
Again the twinkle. He pointed
to huge vats marked
HOPE, DREAMS, LOVE

"We call it the Hallmark section.
A bit saccharine, but that's the point.
Gravity, Mr. Goldberg, is the important thing.
What's at bottom, what is real:
You exist for these devices
and they exist for you."

I can't tell you how happy I felt.
I wanted to see so much more
and then I had to say it.

"This is what I have always wanted,
my dream come true.
It's like I died and went to..."
Again, those twinkling blue eyes.

Ever After

Pinocchio moved out on his sixteenth
birthday and went back to the theater.
He blamed Geppetto for making him
too short for basketball,
too light for football and
generally plain.

The Princes had a hard time
with Snow White and Sleeping Beauty.
They never understood why their kisses
lost power, but, being Princes,
they stayed with the listless women
until the princelings and
princesses went off to college.

Hansel and Gretel were acquitted when
their parents' bones were found in the family furnace,
but no one wanted to take them in.
She wound up on Seventh Avenue;
his whereabouts are unknown.

Cinderella turned out o.k., but what she did
to her stepmother and stepsisters –
the Prince's castle had 300 rooms to keep clean,
not counting the dungeon.

Red Riding Hood's lousy judgment
continued through four marriages,
countless affairs and
forty-five years of inappropriate dress.

I guess the only success story
was Ariel, the Little Mermaid.
Hobbling shakily on her new legs,
she learned to be content with
two-dimensional travel.

I am told that she would leave Eric's bed
and slip down to the shore
to count the stars
and the waves.

And if she dropped a salt tear
into the sea, her sea,
the funny thing is
she called it happiness.

And Call Me in the Morning

This poem is available by prescription only.
Read it once before bed and then as needed.
On advice of counsel, we list the following
warnings and contraindications:

*Use only as directed. As with all verse, excessive
reading may cause boredom and over-analysis.
Do not operate heavy machinery while reading.
Unpredictable reaction when read during
consumption of alcohol or narcotics may lead to
overstimulation, unanticipated coupling and
pregnancy. Or not. Effect may change when read
with other poetry, including greeting card verse and
experimental prose poems. Contact poet immediately
if reading leads to sensation of longing (see alcohol
warning, above).*

So:
I love you.

There it is, 97.5% pure.
Uncut, unbuffered. Yours.
Available only to you, by design,
by prescription, by special compounding,
binding the *I* and *you* with the perfect
connector.

I love you.
This poem is available by prescription only.
Uncut. Unbuffered.
Yours.

The Answer

Not the way the moon paints a path across the water
Not the moon, not the water
Not the call of the stars to join them
dancing across a liquid sky
Not the stars
Not the sky

Not the smell of coffee in the morning
Or at brunch on a bathrobe Sunday
Or the colors of the house
Or the quiet of the house before sleep

Not Galatea, Natalie Wood, Diana Rigg,
Britney, Pamela or Cindy
Not my first wife or any other woman
Or the jealous mistress, *War and Peace*,
Gravity's Rainbow, Prufrock, Dry Tortugas
anything by Merwin or Oliver or by
anyone else living or dead

Or the way it was
Or the way it will be
Or poetry
Or history, biology, gravity,
reality

Not any of these
Not all of these

You

Allison Installed a De-Bugging Program in My Laptop Yesterday

It will fix the problems ("bugs")
that have plagued the computer since
my daughter downloaded
that Spongebob Squarepants Screen Saver.

The program will protect against viruses
(also "bugs") and not allow
my infected computer to spread illness
to those others with whom we consort.
        I have no idea what all this means.

But I did note that the new program
proceeded to act like that wasp
that lays eggs in a cicada's body
as it detected and altered or deleted
other bug-eaters already in residence.
It flew about depositing files
throughout my system,
cross-pollinating everywhere it went.
It chirped and buzzed and lit up
like a firefly when it was done.

So now, as I understand it,
my machine and I are safely fumigated,
securely inoculated against
whatever bug-ugly bandit flies
through the Internet to wait in ambush
this bright Sunday morning
as I scroll sleepily from site to site,
cocooned in my bathrobe,
sipping my decaf,

fluttering my innocent,
computer-illiterate self
into the weird, wild web
that is wide as the world

and from whose silken net
I am realizing there is no escape.

I Am Convinced That There Are Colors I Cannot See

One of these days someone will say to me,
"Doesn't the sky look *slor* tonight?"
and I will say, "Huh?"

I will then discover that there are hues
between blue and red and that
for fifty-some years, my blue slacks
have clashed with the *slor* stripes
on what I thought was a white shirt.

Of course, the person who will tell me these things
will be my wife.
Who is very honest now that we are married.
Who is long-suffering for what I lack.
Who almost has me convinced that I am autistic.

I say it's just that I am a guy.
A sensitive guy by most accounts.
But apparently there is something,
some emotional *slor*,
I just don't get.

Which is why I will always be Louie.
Left on the tarmac with Rick
while Ilsa and what's-his-name fly off.
Clever, cynical, lonely
and probably wearing socks that,
like his relationships,
are hopelessly mismatched.

My Story

Susan (not her real name),
Lucia (pronounced loo-SEE-ah) and I
caught the company car to Kennedy.
We made small talk (tiny, really)
as the Russian driver weaved through traffic.
We got to know each other. Susan
was sailing to the Seychelles to sell. Lucia
was leaving for London. Like me she
was going home.

But only Susan got there on time so Lucia
and I got a drink and settled in, hoping
that something would open up on a later flight.
And when we knew we were well and truly effed,
we got well and truly wasted and took our vouchers
to the Marriott, drank some more and spent the night
crawling all over each other.

And she had lovely eyes
and an unlovely English accent, and of course
none of this happened. She caught her plane
and went home, and I caught my plane and went home,
but her name was *Lucia*.
I could not possibly improve on that.

Appraisal

Sir: We have completed our expert appraisal of the referenced Property and, based on comparables, inspection and other criteria typically used by qualified appraisers, are pleased to advise as follows:

The Property was introduced in 1952 and has been generally well maintained, despite substantial wear and tear and a notable lack of attention to its interior during the period 1982-1990 and to its exterior during the subsequent ten years when we understand it was rented out to an unsympathetic tenant.

The foundation is strong and shows no sign of serious weakness.

Trim and finish show definite signs of wear but are not irreparably damaged in any significant respect.

The major systems are generally serviceable, except the following is noted:

HVAC suffers slightly from years of tobacco and other inhalants which have left it slightly weakened. No immediate repair is recommended.

The computerized electrical system is functioning at a relatively high rate of efficiency but is showing sign of memory malfunction, particularly when asked to store domestic data.

The audio system is likewise in acceptable condition but shows a perplexing inability to pick up the sound of high pitched voices, particularly at night.

The plumbing system shows the weaknesses common to properties of similar age.

We are pleased to report that there is no sign of infestation that cannot be addressed, interior rot or serious structural damage. At least not based on a visual exterior inspection.

SUMMARY: Although no longer stylish or in the condition required of prime properties, the Property is serviceable and has good bones. We believe it marketable so long as the owner is patient and his expectations are not unreasonable.

Take Your Clothes Off

I saw you at the airport
and you smiled at me.
I think I might like you,
so take your clothes off.

No, that is not what I mean,
let me rephrase:
take off
your clothes.
There, is that better?

It's just all these distractions,
that second skin dress,
your neon blonde hair,
those s & m eyes;
you look like you smoke cigarettes,
the long, thin ones.

Makeup, beauty, sex,
how can I know for sure
if I like you?
Those eyes.
Those high, high heels.
Those lips.
Those shoes.

Wherein Our Hero Returns to the Dating Scene

Of course you know
I look this way
to put you at ease.

You might come over here.
Closer. We would have a drink.
Talk about
whatever you would like:
the team
the time
books/movies/music.

We would go to my place
or yours.
I would make love to you
if you'd like.

And then
it would be my turn
to choose.

But not tonight.
Lucky for you
I've already eaten.

Upgrade

NW 1195, Boston to Atlanta 5/6/03

Because he was too slow
on the eTicket machine buttons
poor Ken couldn't upgrade to First Class as I did.
He's back there somewhere, with the po' folks,
the ones who are traveling to see newborn grandkids,
or Key West for the first time, while I
glide effortlessly through the clouds,
the airways greased with a complimentary Bloody Mary,
a Captain of Industry in Seat 5-D.

I look about the cabin for the sneak-thief who got Ken's seat.
Is it the fat, bald burgher in 2-A
drinking his second pre-lunch Scotch
even before we lift off?

Is it one of the Golf Guys in 3-A or B
sharing a chuckle over the putts they missed yesterday
or something about Debi, who dots the "i"
with a plump, expectant heart
and told them that she is a grad student at B.U.
as she danced on their table last night?
I bet they bought her a $500 bottle of champagne,
along with Debi's serious eye contact
telling them they were special.

Or maybe it's Renata in 5-C, whose elbow is touching mine
as she continues to talk on her cell phone
(even though the doors are shut)
about her trip from Boston to Hong Kong

paid for by her travel agency as a perk and, no doubt,
a reward for exemplary service.

I am, God help me, forced to eavesdrop on her while
she does irreparable damage to the plane's
navigation system with her cell signal,
interrupting vectors and ground speed algorithms,
putting our lives at risk
   with something Cindy just has to hear
   about rain in Cat Cay this time of year.
I wonder if the Golf Guys would find her attractive?

As soon as the 767 lifts off, I will
order another free Bloody Mary. How nice
to have a drink named after you,
even if it memorializes mass murder.
How nice to fly free to Hong Kong and
advise your friends on world travel issues.

How nice to upgrade to First Class
for only $50 or some Frequent Flyer Miles.
How nice to believe, at that level
men reserve for such things,
that you have paid $140
for nude dances to a woman who yearns
to run off with you
for a weekend of guilt-free sex
and only you, only you.

Delta Connection

DL 1891, Chicago to Atlanta

Although we have been painstakingly screened,
profiled and judged safe in our flat, non-
threatening pan-Anglican features
by the cheerful government-paid airport staff
in their ill-fitting paramilitary uniforms;

although we have herded ourselves in,
strapped ourselves down,
mouthed the familiar mantra
of FAA-mandated safety precautions
and accepted our duties as exit row wardens,
yet our fingers

foment social revolution.
They intertwine beneath the armrest and slide outside
the pre-assigned boundaries of 27D and 27E,
inflamed with the memory of last night's campaign
beyond all past allegiance,
all restraint, all inhibition.

They are committed to the Cause, these bold digits
that remember earlier irreverence, they who have
torn the tags off mattresses,
raised in solitary salute to fellow drivers,
pointed out the flaws in professors' logic
and so lately traversed the landscapes of our bodies.

Now, empowered, inspired,
they tease the *Che* of the imagination
as another hand reaches for a blanket

and two pairs of insurrectionist eyes
dance in triumph at 10,000 feet,
and climbing.

Write Your Own Damned Title
I Am Too Busy Getting Divorced
Again

I am packing
> *Does this shirt make*
> *my eyes bluer?*
to go to read poetry
> *I read somewhere that*
> *women prefer boxer briefs*
in Columbus, Georgia
and thinking maybe I will meet
> *I guess it never hurts*
> *to bring a few of these,*
> *Boy Scout!*
someone I can talk to.

Perhaps someone from the local college
who is interesting, sensitive,
built. And has a thing for
old, bald men who are
sixty cheeseburgers north of buff.
I have been to this movie before.

I will, at best, smile as I
moonwalk away from someone
roughly my own certain age,
a handsome lady whose time is worth my own.

At worst it will be another future ex
on the insane side of crazy
and I will walk the wrong way.

Still, as I work on yet another
severance pay arrangement,
I obsess over whether these shoes look
too gay and those too macho,
consider removing my wedding ring

a few weeks before the gavel falls
and try to forget that Ma said,
Water seeks its own level,
and the third Chinese curse,
May you find what you are looking for,
follows the bit about
interesting times.

Father

My sister and I thought he was a bear—
usually surly, returning home only
to hibernate, feed and growl.
A bear with a belt in his hand
that one time she sassed him.
He really put his back into it.
I resolved to be careful with words
and later went to law school.

But we never lacked for direction,
and when the house was dark,
after he kissed us good night with his
ursine beard and ordered us to sleep,
when our lesser fears rose
from coffin or castle to lurk at our windows,
it was good to know he was outside the door.

That was fifty years ago, and tonight, as I debate
a third martini, not really wanting
to go home to my wife,
Crystal the cocktail waitress
winks at me.

And Dad, Ol' Bear, I hear you growl
and of course I ask for the check.

All Men are Dogs

egg sucking dog
dope sniffing dog
blackdog
smack dog
mack dog
matter-of-fact dog
blunt dog
hunt dog
runt dog

(other dog)
ubi sunt dog?
all men are dogs for something

big dog
pig dog
want-a-big-rig dog
hog dog
dog dog
modern-day blog dog

other dog

mud dog
bud dog
druggie drugged drug dog
lover dog
mother dog
sister-loving brother dog

always there are other dogs
always there's another dog

name dog
blame dog
they may seem the same dog
hot dog
bot dog
bored until they rot dog
that is what I'm not dog
you are but I'm not dog
this is what I've got dog
always there's another dog
always there's an other dog

Look at That Girl

I need to go
on a diet
and lose twenty years

Elegy

you
interrupt
my loneliness
and I
cannot forgive
you
my loneliness
and I
cannot forgive
you
I cannot forgive
you my
loneliness
interrupt
my loneliness
I cannot
forgive
my loneliness
I cannot
interrupt
my loneliness
I cannot
give you
my loneliness
forgive

Mens Rea

*"Mens Rea" is the intention to do evil that must be proved
for convictions in certain crimes, such as first degree murder.*

...*intent?*
not really
I just want to get
from A to C
and B should watch out

*****

when I was a boy
I wasn't

*****

I know how to discipline kids
first you beat them 'til they cry
then you beat them 'til they stop

*****

How could you kill all those people?
They were human beings!

not anymore

*****

but don't worry, I wouldn't kill you
and I couldn't hide the body if I did

*****

We should read this interview
to our kids

just read them a bedtime story
where Goldilocks
gets ate

Hero

You are equal to your dreams.

You have done all
that you hoped to do, eventually.

You stand, your feet flecked
with dragon blood, your wings
drenched with moon dust,

the satisfied angel cooing in your bed,
her dark-eyed twin draped over the ottoman,

your minions outside the palace door
and death slinking away
battered and bruised but grinning
slyly I suppose, knowing
you will call her name
soon enough.

Thanksgiving

Uncle Morty is late and smells of why.
We assume Aunt Kate won't make it
again this year. It takes an Act of Congress
to get Freddie, home from college, to stop
text messaging and come to the table.
He's intent on reaching
someone named John.
Aunt Bev doesn't want to talk about it.

The twins are pissed about being at
the kiddie table and let everyone know.
Grandpa doesn't like the diagnosis on his hip
or the gravy. My wife turns off the TV
with the grim finality of a guillotine
but it's only the Lions after all.
Cousin Tim complains he needs it on
in case al Qaeda attacks.

Then, as if on cue in a Capra movie,
we bow our heads,
Grandma mumbles something familiar
and as one we *Amen* and reach for the dressing.

Big Night

"To eat beautiful food is to know God."

No doubt about it, I think,
as I add a bit of garlic and hold off on
the basil until the very last moment,
there is something way sensual here.

All the *oni*s and *ini*s, *oros* and *iti*s,
linguini luxuriating on the plate,
the rich, red pomodoro sauce
vibrant with basil, marjoram, garlic and pepper.
No doubt about it, these people
can really cook.

Culingioni, my Mu-zarella, I propose, knowing
that no woman's honor can withstand my
Penne, al dente, di Vitello.
Pecorino, you smirk at me, *Chianti,*
Brunello, Rosso,
Barolo,

Focaccio, I threaten, *Bracioli Ripieni di Rape,*
Fegato, you accuse playfully, *Stufato di Manzo*
Funghi, I snarl back, but of course

everything will soon be *Gnocchi,*
we'll *Zampone* as the bed squeaks
and the neighbors wonder
at the shouting:

Osso Bucco!
Mascarpone!
Pasta!
Pasta!
Pasta!

Patriotica

When we love we are like all the people
coming together to make America.

We are Manifest Destiny, the great exploration,
boldly going where no white one went before,
Lewis and Clark, Sacagawea, Pocahontas,
Geronimo! Wagons Ho! Walt Whitman, Horace Greeley,
Opening of the West! Go, Young Man!

And when we love, we are like every battle hymn
of our Republic, drunk with our freedom.
Jingoists, super-national patriots, I won't go down
with the ship that has not yet begun to fight,
I won't fire until I see the whites of your eyes;
we are the majesty of the purple mountains,
the waving amber grains, oh say, see
and trip the light fantastic, I sing America.

Oh, when we love we are like
all the people coming together to make
America. I am Superman and Paul Bunyan,
you are surely Wonder Woman and Ms. Liberty.
We lay our hands across the sea, make
one nation under God and indivisible,
your Presbyterian and my Jew melding together
in that Great Molten American Pot conceived and dedicated
of, by and for the people from sea to shining sea
and truly America the Beautiful.

Empathy for Hitler

Because my wife said I would write better poetry
if I could put myself in someone else's skin and really,
really, really feel what they feel.

And now the workday is over
and I am clearing the dishes.
The children are watching a movie about a man
who enters a dense forest, a sword in his hand.
And I am that man as I put
each spaghetti-encrusted fork on its plate.
My heart pounds and I adjust my helmet.
I am about to stride into the forest
when suddenly I am the forest.
I am dark, deep, numb with age,
indifferent to the lives within me.

When I turn and carry the dishes to the sink,
glancing at my daughter's painting
of a crouching panther, I feel the hairs on my back rise
and the hunger grow within me.
I can scarcely contain my need to leap through the window
and go on a delicious, tense prowl.
Mrs. Cochran's Westies are in serious jeopardy.
If only you would call.

I turn on the faucet, set the temperature,
measure out the soap. If only you would call, soon,
I might stop myself from being the water.
From doing my work on the sauce
and pasta and ground beef,
then hurling myself down the drain.
Please call because if you do not,
I will flow down, then through the sewer,

past the rats and possible crocodiles,
and then, without you as my focus,
I will become the sea.

Oh Lordy, Lord, my Darling
we can't have that!
I will roil and rise and
heave up my back against the stars
and spread out all the way to China.

China?
Oh, please call.
It is very boring here.
And I am afraid.

Recipes from the Book of Creation

1.

Let's start with something simple:
Cats.
Sinew is the word (remembering always
that the selection of the right word
is the first essential ingredient).

Sinews and mews.
Like a dog, but without
the rough edges.
Stretch the dog
and your thought of dog.

It will learn to say
its true name;
that is how you will know
when it's done.

2.

Light is much more difficult.
No sound, you know, and
too many words coming too close:
heat
       bright
             glimmer
close but never quite right.

You cannot rush this one.
Light will quicken
in its own belly.
Skip the usual and start
with what light can do:
what your plants need
so they won't spoil,
what turns the faces,
       browns the flesh,
            closes the iris,
                opens the bud.

Lay these out and wait
for the reaction to do your work.

3.

Love?
Harder still.
You must start beyond formula,
          beyond cause and effect.

Love is friction.
Rub together the words you
find within yourself, but
be careful.

Love will rise
and spread outside your kitchen,
creating and recreating itself,
out of control.

It will fill the whole house
with its leavening strength
and burst your doors.

Be sure to break off a piece
and save it as a starter
for your next batch.

Muse

Eagle, perched on his aerie,
prayed to his god, the wind:
"Oh, lift me high in your embrace
that I may soar for hours and catch many fish."

Fish, sinking deeper, prayed
to his god, the ocean:
"Please hold me safe that I do not
fall prey to the scuttling things beneath
or disappear into the glare above."

Ocean prayed to its god, the moon:
"Guide my ebb and flow that I may grow
even more beautiful,
as your invisible hands
stroke my back each night."

Moon prayed to the sun:
"Hide not your brilliance from me."
And Sun prayed to its god
who prayed to its
and so on, even as Old Kettle Eyes
threw her bones and prayed:
"Oh carry me on your feathered wings
that I may fly to heaven and be one
with Moon and Sun and Wind and all things."

And Wind, who had no god,
laughed in its empty heart and blew joyfully
in daylight and darkness,
over sea and sand,
through everything,
making only music.

Why I Write

The most annoying thing is the way
they sneak up on you when you least expect.
On a crowded, sweaty bus
>   **"Poem"**
over there, behind the fat lady
or the guy in the polyester . . .
>   **"Poem, hey, over here,
>   Poem"**
So you try to turn away,
but it follows you and
at the grocery, among the fish sticks
>   **"Poem!"**
At work, in the middle **("Poem")** of a
rush **("Poem!")** project **("POEM!")**
And just before sleep
>   **"poemmmm."**
Or making love that should be
chapter and verse enough
>   **"Poem!"**
("Not now, for heaven's sake!")
>   **"Poem! Poem! Poem!"**

And for all of it, the word, the word that keeps
puppy-jumping into your consciousness,
insistent, self-certain, joyously seductive,
sprawls herself naked upon the page,
sated, spent and small
and not what you thought she'd be at all.

And then, even as the page is crumpled
and cast out
with the cigarette butts
and beer cans,
a sly, sweet,
red delicious voice
calls

> **"Pssst.**
> **Over here.**
> **In the garbage.**
>
> **Poem."**

Lay Lake

Leah Ellen Marks 12/2/90 - 12/7/07

How John and I are fishing,
despite everything.
Because of everything.

How you find bass
where the shore and the weeds
and a fallen log make structure.
Not out in the open water.

How John has caught a bass
and I have not.

There is so much I would show you.

How the mist glides over Lay Lake
and two men,
the men who loved you,
the men who failed you,
sit in their little boat, one talking,
the other silent within himself.

How this lake is bound
by shores, by trees,
by land that is bound
only by the sky and the sky
and the sky.

Aftermath

When you told me to get out, your anger
punched a hole through our marriage;
a black spot hung in the air
in the kitchen, in between us.

When I looked to you, it obscured your face,
so I tried walking to the side, but it was still there,
a black spot as big as your fist.

It made a sucking sound
and began to grow.

My first thought was to find something
to plug it up, yours, to your credit,
was for the children who you loaded into the car
and drove off, leaving me with the blackness
as it swelled into the dining room.

I ran upstairs for a Bible
but when I turned around
it was advancing up the steps and
it backed me into the bedroom,
into the closet, into a corner and
all I could see was black so I knew
it was on me and I closed my eyes
and held my breath but I had to
breathe so I inhaled and when

I opened my eyes the lights were on
and everything was back the way it should be.

At least that's what I thought,
damn you,
until I looked in the mirror.

Covenant

Let us face each day with at least
        the nervous courage
                of the king's food taster.

Let us never leave dishes in the sink

and make the beds each morning
        to show the police
                that we survived the initial blast.

Let us agree never to speak of things that matter.

Let us share faith that there is a home
        for misplaced keys, second
                socks and favorite toys,

and also for unsaid words
        missed opportunities
                and lost children.

That, like confessions, prayers need not be shouted
        or even voiced
                to be heard.

That there is no need for periods in grammar or time.

That there is more to us than this
        and that we are less
                than something more,

but let us agree to share wonder wordlessly

and to face each day with the force
that binds one sudden moment
to the next.

Else

Lunge. The frog becomes
part of the snake.
Bite, hold and the springbok
is part of the lioness, her cubs.
Bits of me
are parts of mosquitoes and
smaller bits now dissolve into
smaller predators.

My daughter is now
part of time, an appendage of memory.
What she lost was the part of her
that is not part of me.

*****

Myself, I am still here, my self
selfishly refusing to go,
to be part of anything else.

I feel the bridges burn,
the bowline slip, the tethers release.
I am being lost to you.

I have forgotten our first date,
your birthday, how
to make you laugh.

I am forgetting that I love you.

*****

What shall I do with this knowledge?
Explore whether the frog becomes part
of the hawk that eats the snake?
Declare that memory is richer
for the children it consumes?

Or shall I simply throw out an *I'm sorry*
and let go of it all,
falling away to become smaller,
smaller and then something
altogether else?

Sigh

less than the light
less than the clouds
less even than
the ephemeral smile
when you were my halcyon child

less than the poem
I meant to write
that now escapes me our joy
flared and faded
leaving not even a wisp of itself

and so will the sorrow
that shoots a susurrus
but cannot be reduced to the page

it lingers for second
and then recedes

impermanent as sound

A Prayer of Appreciation
for the Lesser Gods

Goddess of the afternoon nap,
god of the rhymed couplet,
mischievous god of the lost other sock,
grinning goddess of yummy,
    I don't even know your names;

Boo Goo, god of nonsense words,
You Too, god of yawns,
Oh My god of simultaneous orgasms
(son of Aphrodite and Asperg, god of
precise timepieces),

        I imagine you in patio homes
        down the way from Olympus,
        not godly enough
        to be employed full time,
        you spend the odd hours
        in sideshows,
        doing kids' parties,
        whatever keeps you in
        nectar and ambrosia
        or maybe Hershey's miniatures

F Word, god of curses that
result in fistfights,
Gimme, goddess of ex-wives,
and *Wat-tha?*, god of dangerous distraction,

        To you I would sacrifice a hamster
        or perhaps Chia Pet
        or at least toss a quarter into a well,

not for personal gain,
but explanation for my missing brown sock
and the momentary lapse last week
that resulted in a fender bender
too human for notice by *Zeus,*
or even *Hephaestus.*

Dog Soldier

At night the dogs come to me.
They sit around the fire
and I tell them my stories.

I know that some are wolves
clothed as dogs
and vice versa.

Occasionally, one of the imposters
will silently work his way
around behind me, lunge
and bury his teeth in my shoulder.

I will reach with my other arm,
tear him off and toss him
into the fire.
He will howl,
then whimpering drag himself
into the shadows to die.

I do not mind.
He does not mind.
We are dogs.
This is what we do.

*****

A dog must learn
three things:
>   his name,
>   the way home,
>   not to mount
>   the big dog's mate.

The rest is instinct.

*****

Stallions forced from a herd
must live alone,
wandering the prairies.

The same is true
for wild dogs.

The Apache, Cheyenne
and Kiowa called
their fiercest horsemen
Dog Soldiers.

*****

The quiet one caught my eye
from the first. She was my type.
Sweet-faced, shy.
Well bred.

We talked above the music
as best we could.
Then we went somewhere quiet
and spoke of old lovers
husbands and wives.
Of dreams we once had.

I am waiting for her to wake
so I can fix her breakfast
and see her home.
I will call her again
and we will, I suppose,
"date" for a time.
I will tell her my stories
and she will tell me hers.

And at some point,
there will be no point
to our being together and
we will part.
She will not mind, really.
And I will not mind.

Allow Me

To take your place in the exit row

To walk with you to baggage claim

To light your cigarette

To give you a lift

To show your wife the door

To make the bed   after

To open and organize your mail

To update your password

To accept in your honor

       your promotion

       your prize

       your eulogy

To prove that lives are

       fungible commodities

To explain this to you as I

            try on your coat

To love your life

To introduce you   to oblivion

I Should Tell You This

On the morning after the night
I fell in love with you, I woke
and heard an owl,
the first since I moved in-town.

Perhaps he was just trying to panic
some mouse from its hiding place,
to bring it into the surrendering dark,
claim its life and bear it away from itself.

Perhaps he was calling to a mate
real, imagined or departed.

Most likely, he was chanting his own name,
in the joy and fullness of his being,
singing his name against the sun,
who was blazing its name
against the moon, who,
retreating gracefully,
was whispering its name against the hours.
And I thought,

This is how we love—
we find something so beautiful
it astonishes us.

We grasp it and clutch it so tightly as
to cleave it to us and hope
it does not break.

We press against it our lives,
our joys, our ugliness,

the heat and talons and small graces,
the appetites and sorrows that
we know of ourselves. We push
and pray that it does not let us go.

An Alabama Christmas Wish

There should be snow
because we live apart.
There should be snow so
it will be more like Christmas.

There should be snow to fur
the trees with cold crystal down
and let us keep track of our steps,
to dust our heads and give
substance to the air,
to make walking an adventure.

There should be snow for the sake
of 4-wheel drive SUVs
and as an insult to the other ones.
There should be snow to make people
put down shopping bags and use their arms
for better things.

There should be snow so that my daughters
will have a hot chocolate/comic book
day off from school, so that the city
will be Currier and Ived, a happy postcard
where cars don't work, chimneys smoke,
and the 21st Century gives it a rest.

There should be snow
for snowmen
and snow angels
and snowball wars,
and it tastes good, too.

There should be snow to shrink
our overbig world
of too many options,
too many miles,
too many differences between your Christian
and my Jew, your tree and my menorah
to one warm welcome home,
one room, one fireplace
and the Christmas we make
in each other's arms.

How We Die

Little bits of us evaporate into the sky.
Little bits of us are sucked into the earth.
Little bits of us are nibbled off.
Always wear a hat.
Always wear shoes.
Never wear shorts, tank tops.
Never go out without gloves,
and never let anyone touch you.

If you have a thought, do not speak it
or the sky will take it and make it great.
Or the earth will take it to feed an iris.
Or a woman will take it for a poem.

Listen to me and you
will live forever, you will
keep yourself whole, you will.

Listen to me, I just spent seven hours
at a family wedding.
Not my family.
My wife's family.
I have lost four hundred twenty minutes,
seventeen ounces.
I have longed for death
as a lady in pearls told me

about someone's cancer,
someone's divorce.

Listen to me, groom.
Listen to me, ring-bearer.

Time and life and lizard's tail.
Only one of these grows back.

Laying Track for Noah

Thomas the Really Useful Tank Engine
comes with a standard figure-eight track.
But of course, that is not enough.

We have purchased Thomas Friends Percy and James,
Duncan and Molly, and Emily and Harvey.
We own the Sodor Line Roundhouse and the Secret Mine.
We operate our very own drawbridge.

But we need more track to avoid Island of Sodor gridlock,
so I am hard at work expanding the 8.
I invite Noah to watch as I add sweeping arcs
of right-and-left-curving track, showing him how they fit.
He wants to do it himself, but that would lead to disaster
at the wide-grilled furnace register or the basement stairs.

Laying track is a man's job,
even a man who never cared for tracks
or nonviolent toys that ran on them,

and I remember how Dad,
working at the flight hospital in Korea,
filled the hours between surgeries and stitchings
building HO trains from kits he bought at the PX.

Home, he gleefully assembled a twenty-six car train,
complete with locomotive, caboose and eight feet of circular track.
I am told that I watched for a minute, and then toddled away.
He threw out the set.

But Noah loves trains and,
while I question my fitness for the job,
I lay track and love my son.

Thomas the Really Useful Tank Engine
comes with a standard figure-eight track.
But of course, that is not enough.

Little Soul

"'Little soul,' says Epictetus, 'bearing about a corpse'"
—David Bottoms, O Mandolin, O Magnum Mysterium

Tiny, really.
So small you can escape
through the hole a virus shoots through flesh.

Incorporeal,
yet strong enough to carry the rest of me
through the obstacle course of my days,
shrinking from the mirror,
roiling as we pass meadow or lake.

Do I lose a piece of you
each time I open the mail?
Are you buried beneath the sand-
slow hours of every unblessed day?

I know only that by day you
strain to make yourself known,
and I imagine that you flee
my snores each night
to sit on the windowsill,
inhale moonlight and starshine
and swell with wonder

before returning to lift your heavy load,
sodden with life,
while you whisper to muscle and bone,

There is more,
there is always more.

About the Author

Barry Marks is a Birmingham attorney whose poetry, fiction, articles and essays have been published in nearly 100 journals, magazines and periodicals over the last 30 years. Mr. Marks was 1998 Alabama State Poetry Society Poet of the Year and his chapbook, *There is Nothing Oppressive as a Good Man,* won the Society's 2003 Morris Chapbook Competition. His full-length collection, *Possible Crocodiles,* won the Society's Book of the Year Award in 2010. A member of the Big Table Poets, his work is featured in that group's anthologies, *Poems from the Big Table* and *Einstein at the Odeon Cafe.* He is a past president of the Alabama State Poetry Society and a former Board member of the Alabama Writer's Conclave.

Please visit Brick Road Poetry Press at our web site
for more poetry collections
that will entertain, amuse, and edify:
www.brickroadpoetrypress.com

BRICK ROAD
POETRY PRESS

In the following pages, samples are provided from
Dancing on the Rim by Clela Reed,
Damnatio Memoriae by Michael Meyerhofer
& *Drunken Robins* by David Oates.

Dancing on the Rim by Clela Reed

ISBN-13: 978-0-9841005-0-7

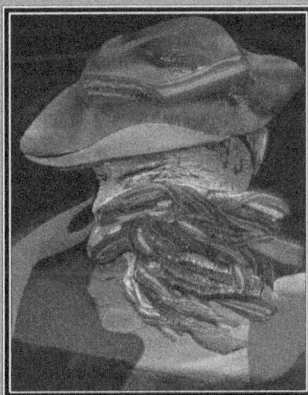

Dancing on the Rim
Poems
Clela Reed

From *Dancing on the Rim* by Clela Reed

The Princess Regrets Ever After

And then one day she found she missed
the old enchantment. Oh, being swept away
was nice enough—the jewels, his gathering arms,
the carriage ride, the sheer surprise (imagine!).
She adored the wedding and his doting charm,
but eventually she found the prince's skin
too warm to the touch, too smooth, that he
lacked the intriguing bumps, their patterns
beneath her fingertips like messages of devotion
in Braille, that his lidded eyes merely blinked
in their bony hollows instead of watching her
from top-most ridge, beneath delicate shades
lowering and rising in time to her breathing,
that his legs though long seemed lacking
in a certain strength and grace as he stroked
his father's lake, his fluttering kicks annoying
the fish. A leap was beyond him and diving
to the depths to retrieve for her…well, that
would never happen. And she came to dislike
the sound of his voice, its raspy tweedle, devoid
of the full-throated pitch that rattled the river reeds
and claimed nocturnal rule. But mostly she found that
at night upon her satin pillow when his fleshy lips
found hers, she closed her eyes and thought
of the slick-rimmed mouth, the cool scent of the pond,
the irresistible tickle of a fly-snatcher's tongue.

From *Dancing on the Rim* by Clela Reed

Seducing Newton

Once I start, I stay in motion,
revolve about his body as I loosen
his cravat, empty his pockets of coins,
old apples, small rockets, and brush
his hair until the long fall shines
in waves of corpuscular light.
He calls me his merry moon;
I call him my knight.

I purr, "Isaac, dear,
if I give you a little shove
onto the chaise, will you resist,
equally?" He grants me his
Royal Minted smile, sterling grade,
but regains gravitas as I fluff the pillows,
snuff the candle, pull the shade.

And here let me say only that
with sweetest force we accelerate
to enlightenment, and through
our own algorithms, I persuade him
to fathom what cannot be charted and weighed
or found in the sky through ground-lens precision,

that a pulse of white light can explode into colors
without passing first through a prism,
that sometimes the ripe apple that falls
to the ground and rolls to your feet
is there just to eat.

From *Dancing on the Rim* by Clela Reed

Saturday Cartoons

You know how when a reckless 'toon
takes two steps too far into air,
high up, unaware,
and stays suspended there,
silly look on coyote face (or duck-
billed or dog-eared or pig-nosed mug)
or just dumb-fuck
human dude?
You know how it hits him then—
light's on, damn-I'm-screwed—
and he pedals the air?

There. That's where I am, right there,
gone too far, realizing at last,
nothing to do but give up and fall.
And I won't bounce back after the crash,
stars and birdies haloing my head, and you above,
against a yellow sky, one radiant gleam
from your toothy grin.

From *Dancing on the Rim* by Clela Reed

Lagniappe

It's the way we place the best peach
on the kitchen sill in morning sun,
knowing flesh and juice
beneath its velvet
will distill
soil, water,
blossom and light
into sweetness.

So when we eat it,
striking gold and rose
below inviting skin,
dripping nectar
down our limbs,
licking clean the stone,
we consume in swollen
hemispheres
one tender blend,
one peach's universe.

In just this way I've placed
my love for you
in the window of myself
sunniest spot,
distilling all that shines
in the calling world I roam
into a ripened sweetness,
globe of flavor
you will one day taste,
you may one day
even savor.

Damnatio Memoriae by Michael Meyerhofer

ISBN-13: 978-0-9841005-5-2

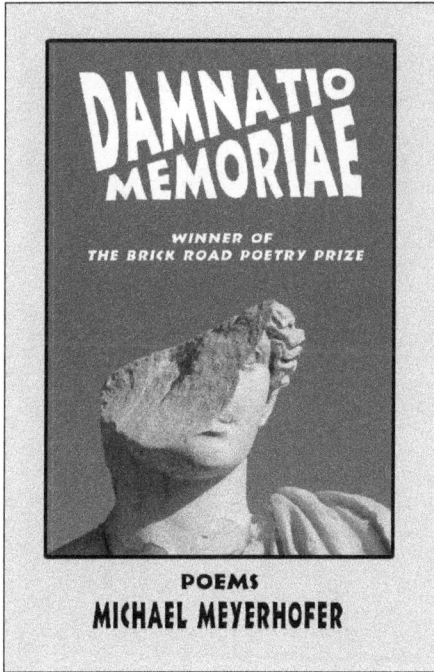

From *Damnatio Memoriae* by Michael Meyerhofer

Betting on the Wrong Horse

If a train moves southwest at eighty miles an hour
while another train moves northeast at half that speed,
and it's Tuesday, what's your favorite color?

I suppose I should tell you I think
sleep counts as a form of attempted suicide,
especially if dreams of hot air balloons

weaving through power lines are involved.
If you happen to be a fan of getting bitten
by snakes, you probably already know not to try

and suck out the poison, despite what Hollywood says.
I think this is important because at the moment,
I'm listening to Mozart so I can write

I'm listening to Mozart and maybe appear
a bit sultry and cultured, despite my pale background
of factory lines and hand-me-down

campers parked in the shadow of Iowa cedars.
On the day my mother died, I walked along the river
because I wanted to be alone, but didn't mind

when my uncle's Labrador padded after me—
the one killed by a pickup blaring Charlie Daniels
a summer or two later. The black Lab,

that is. Not my uncle, who still smokes
pot to stay sane for lack of therapy and pills.
Sometimes he walks along the same river

that ravels below abandoned train tracks,
looking for arrowheads washed up by the current.
He knows what is hidden never stays that way.

From *Damnatio Memoriae* by Michael Meyerhofer

Dedication

In our house, not once did we hear
someone say *you're welcome*
in answer to thanks. Instead—*it's all right,*
backhanded reminder of the sacrifice
this or that Dollar Store trinket
cost folks well below the poverty line.
This is a hard habit to break.
Don't worry, it's fine when you thank me
for helping you move furniture
or coming to your reading,
your wedding, your beloved's funeral.
Oh, it's all right, to students
when they thank me for margin comments,
for letting them turn in assignments
half a semester late. *It's all right*—
the door held open a few seconds longer
for the jock on crutches,
for the blue-eyed girl breathing
into the straw fixed to her wheelchair.
I want to thank the moon for tilting
in time to highlight the rain
spilling off a parked windshield,
my body for keeping itself free
so far from cancer, diabetes, suicide.
I want to thank my fear of death
for melting whenever a beautiful woman
bends to drink from a fountain.
I want to thank the crows for mating

on any windowsill but mine.
And their answer, rising in chorus
with each day's rusty sunset:
It's all right. It's all right. It's all right.

From *Damnatio Memoriae* by Michael Meyerhofer

Buying an Ice Scraper

Down past underwired mannequins,
aisles beyond the red tubes of buckshot
but before the Disney pacifiers,

I find them arrayed like minutemen—
midnight-blue, green as wormwood,
arm-length ones with bristles,

stubby ones sold two for ten bucks,
faces tipped like Japanese fans.
That easily, I am back in Osage, Iowa,

winter of my fourteenth year,
helping my brother scrape the ice
off the windshield of Dad's '77 Granada

with an empty Bon Jovi tape case,
wondering as I watched our breath rise
to curse the morning snowfall

gowning maples older than I was,
why life wasn't easier. Hundred below
with wind-chill, heater busted,

a sense already that in time
it could get worse. Later, as our father
withdrew the insulin needle

from our mother's blue forearm,
without turning, he asked us
why we hadn't looked under the seat.

From *Damnatio Memoriae* by Michael Meyerhofer

Apologia

Those days when she found herself
banking on the alchemical grace
of a hemodialysis machine
that, quite literally, withdrew her lifeblood
a gulp at a time then routed it back,
freshly laundered, my brother and me
killed time at the coin shop down the street.
It did not seem strange to us,
that little hole-in-the-wall
where a war vet sold wheat pennies
for two cents, mint silver dollars
in clear plastic sleeves.
I recall a Mason jar of Buffalo Nickels
like the kind we'd sometimes
kick up on the river road,
faintly glinting in our footsteps.
The British fifty pence; the Hong Kong
two-dollar with its ruffled edges;
bright, two-tone pesos; and oddest of all
to farm boys with nothing to do,
Japanese coins with holes in the middle—
For string, the man said. *Just in case
you don't have pockets.* And it never entered
my mind to bring her back a necklace,
a kind of garish copper garland
she'd wear once she could walk again.
Once she was done trying
to laugh off the shock of being drained
down to her last drop of commerce,
never once asking us to stay.

Melancholia

After my mother's diabetes finally made me
half an orphan, my father and I drove north through
the white uppercuts of an Iowa snowstorm
to catch a plane to Fort Lauderdale,
then a cruise ship bound for the Bahamas.
My father saw the ad on late nite cable—
a day in Florida, plus two nights on the ocean.
All free, but not really. The boat rocked
like a drunken buoy, hefting shrimp scampi
from so many passengers that the crew tacked
barf-bags to the carpeted walls. No single women
under fifty, anyway. One afternoon, anchored
at the straw market in Nassau, honey-brown children
sold us Bob Marley tee-shirts made in Taiwan.
Then off to Blue Lagoon Island, a Caribbean speck
Hollywood forgot. A sign said they filmed
Gilligan's Island here, a few decades before broken
bottles and tourist shacks bled the place dry,
so that not even the ocean's raised skirts
could save us. I wandered like an astronaut
on bleach-tone sands, found my first native coconut,
read some D.H. Lawrence in a hammock
and spent the next twenty-four hours itching.
But at least this gave me a better reason
to turn down the kind advances of the gay
lookout, whose apparent job it was
to keep his eyes peeled for Caribbean icebergs.
I would like to end here by saying
some epiphany wriggled its way out of this,
maybe some analogy of death and consumerism

mitigated by me paying witness
to the enduring beauty of coconut trees,
or standing on the top-deck of that tin ship,
breathing—Whitmanesque—the moist night air
until I decided, in time, not to jump.
But I am not a liar, although I play one in real life.
I came home the same. My father remarried.
My mother, whom I love, is still dead.
Sometimes, when I write, I can feel myself
pushing a lawnmower over the space
where her body reaches, quietly, for the sky.

From *Damnatio Memoriae* by Michael Meyerhofer

Climate Change

Maybe death is a party
so good, nobody wanders out for air.
But here, we bandy words
and paper in the weighty pause
between thunderheads.
During the day,
storms darken the sky.
At night, they brighten it..

From *Damnatio Memoriae* by Michael Meyerhofer

The Basics

I was in fifth grade the day the nuns
brought in a nice Catholic doctor
to teach us about reproduction.

The boys, that is. A nurse arrived
to educate the girls while the doctor
herded the rest of us across the hall,

nervously told some jokes, chalked out
an absolutely sexless diagram
that omitted all the important parts.

We left more confused than before.
A few boys didn't even know the basics:
kind of like yours, but inside out,

my aunt said later, changing
her toddler-daughter's diaper while
I shifted balance in the doorway,

wanted to run outside and play
but knew, for the first time in my life,
I was learning something important.

Drunken Robins by David Oates

ISBN-13: 978-0-9841005-1-4

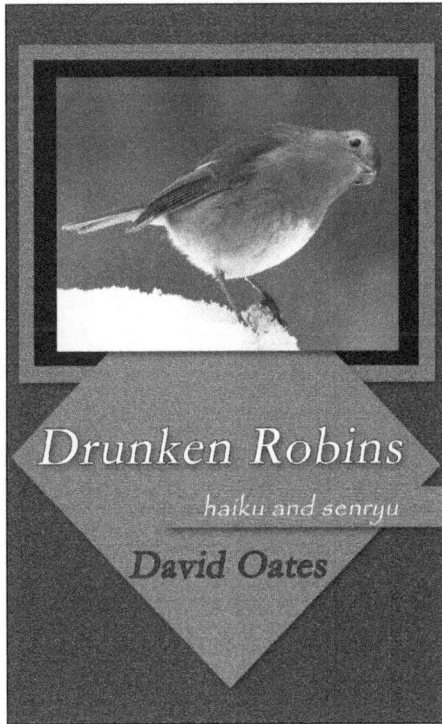

From *Drunken Robins* by David Oates

morning after, driving 65
one aspirin escapes his hand

winter sun—
an old dog sleeps
by the swing set

she's in good spirits
till two weeks after first chemo—
too much hair in the comb

From *Drunken Robins* by David Oates

chemotherapy
she practices drawing on
eyebrows

mountain farmer tends
the burning field's margin
scorched boot smell

engineering classroom
different colored chalk rectangles
on the light brown ceiling

From *Drunken Robins* by David Oates

he teaches Logic and Ethics
never picked for jury

rushing by the scenic overlook—again

older brother, as Easter bunny,
steers the youngest towards eggs
as the middle fills her basket

From *Drunken Robins* by David Oates

little boy sleeps with a smile
bulldozer dream

the sight of home's hills
after a week at the beach
first swallow of wine

rusty old car
decorated today—
"JUST MARRIED"

From *Drunken Robins* by David Oates

gray dawn,
motion-detecting porch light
flicks on
as a catbird hops

after miscarriage
against the wall
a new crib

Times Square
mud puddle
flashing

From *Drunken Robins* by David Oates

the poet conjures angels
in a rolling voice—
his dog loudly, steadily,
licks herself

digging in
his pocket for change
pacifier

in the long grass
by the bird feeder
a cat seems to doze